RIPPLES

RIPPLES

A COLLECTION OF POETIC EXPRESSIONS

BY

GARY FRANKLIN GILLESPIE

www.bookstandpublishing.com

Published by
Bookstand Publishing
Morgan Hill, CA 95037
3662_4

Copyright © 2012 by Gary Franklin Gillespie
All rights reserved. No part of this publication may be reproduced or transmitted in any form or by any means, electronic or mechanical, including photocopy, recording, or any information storage and retrieval system, without permission in writing from the copyright owner.

ISBN 978-1-61863-298-2

Printed in the United States of America

ACKNOWLEDGEMENTS

To the author's family: wife, Marty; son, Shawn; daughter Melanie (husband Todd), daughter Kristie; grandsons Scott, Derrick, Christopher, Shane; granddaughters Sarah, Kara and Elizabeth and many friends, coworkers and acquaintances who have enjoyed Gary's writings over the years and persistently encouraged the publishing of his poetry.

To our dear friend, Larry R. Price, for editing of punctuation and spelling.

Personal comments and background information on some of these poems are those of Gary's wife, Marty, who tried over the years to collect and preserve the hand-scribbled pages of word pictures that flowed from the heart of her husband.

INTRODUCTION

This book is dedicated to the memory of the loving and courageous man who was my husband for forty-seven years and eighteen days: Gary Franklin Gillespie. On June 25, 2010, he had major surgery for a back problem. Three weeks later, on July 16th, a blood clot passed through his heart and into his lungs, and he was gone so quickly. No time for good-byes.

Gary began writing down his thoughts in the form of poetry soon after the birth of our son. Over the years, he would write whenever he felt inspired. His writings are intensely personal; some humorous, others deeply spiritual. His passions come alive as he plays with words to paint a picture of an emotion, a memory, an observation, a truth. At times, when others had an opportunity to read one of his poems and it touched them in some special way, a frequent comment was: "You say what I feel."

Children (all children) held a special place in his heart. He treated the neighborhood kids like he treated his own. One of these, who grew up with our son and was a best friend, sent a letter to me the week after Gary's passing. Following are some excerpts from Scott's letter:

"As I sit here reflecting on the events that have taken place in the past week, I am struck with the reality that the greatest man I have ever known is no longer with us. I reflect on the time that I was able to spend with him, and the lessons I learned from him. He had this ability to make me want to be a better person....He taught me that selflessness was not weakness but strength. I don't know if he was purposely teaching us about human nature, or if I was so awestruck at him that I hung on everything he did and saw the lesson in it....Gary had the ability to treat everyone with respect and dignity even when they deserved a swift kick in the backside. From that I learned to always treat other people the way I want to be treated....He showed me what a father is supposed to be, the father I want to be. He did not teach me everything I learned from him. He showed me. That is more important than any words."

TABLE OF CONTENTS

The Theme — 1
    Ripples — 3

Potpourri — 5
    Begending — 6
    Consider — 7
    The Wish — 8
    The Quiet Way — 10
    They Dream — 11
    Heritage — 12
    Stand Fast, America! — 13
    Ode to Robert — 14
    Frustration — 15
    The Grieving — 16

Family & Friends — 17
    A Father's Delight — 18
    Did You Ever? — 19
    My Little Princess — 20
    Son — 21
    Heaven Sent — 22
    Scotty — 23
    Pappy Roe — 24

Sacred Reflections — 27
    The Beginning — 28
    A Need to Love — 29
    Not Very Big at All — 30
    A Man Died — 31
    The Source — 32
    Overflowing — 33
    A Dark Valley…and Light — 34
    His Face — 35
    Until — 36
    …but Lost — 37

TABLE OF CONTENTS (continued)

Eerie Imaginings   **39**
    The Awakening   41
    The Graveyard   42

Love For A Lifetime   **45**
    Meant to Be   46
    My Love   47
    The Chamber   48
    Here With You   49
    Going Home   51

THE THEME

The poem "Ripples" has always been a favorite and is the theme of this book. It is at the heart of the author whose deep desire was to reach out to others and help those in need.

He once said: "If there's something I write that helps one person, then I think my writing has served its purpose."

RIPPLES

Today I stood upon the shore
   of a place I'd visited many times before.
I cast a pebble into the lake
   and marveled at the responding wake.
Small ripples, round and very neat,
   hastened to shore and vanished at my feet.
Where had they gone? I must find out –
   perhaps a larger stone cast further out.

A repeat of what I'd done before
   brought larger ripples to the shore.
Again I watched as they disappeared
   and brought to pass what I had feared.
A beautiful thought then came to me
   to cast a pebble into an endless sea.
Could the ripples last forevermore
   if there were no restricting shore?

I thought, perhaps, that I could be
   a pebble cast into a human sea.
A show of love to those I touch
   would make my ripples mean so much.

Within our lives are many shores
   that stop the ripples Love outpours.
We're filled with jealousy, hate and strife
   and deprived of Love's ripples in the Sea of Life.
Oh Lord, I pray that we could be
   caught in Love's ripples in an endless sea.
Caught in an endless ripple of Love
   created by a pebble cast from above.

POTPOURRI

(… a sweet medley)

BEGENDING
(Beginning & Ending combined)

There's something I am plagued with,
and have been my whole life through.
It's that of not completing
what I set out to do.

Oh, I have good intentions
with every project I begin;
but I never seem to finish it
or stick with it to the end.

Talk about excuses!
No one has more than me.
Why, I have more excuses
than there are leaves upon a tree.

I work harder at not finishing
the things I try to do
than if I had completed it
and gone on to see it through.

You know, it's hard sometimes completing
the things that you may try.
But it's easy just to walk away
and watch your project die.

Many stories have been written
on success and how it's won;
but you'll never know success, my friend,
until what you start is done.

Do all you can to finish
whatever you may start.
Mix in a little effort.
Blend in a little heart.

Hey! I am now successful!
My life has a brand new trend.
You see...my poem had a beginning,
and now it has an end.

CONSIDER

Perhaps I'm not the greatest thing

that God has ever made.

And I know there are many things I've tried

that didn't make the grade.

I know that I am not so smart;

many things I do not know.

And many times I tried so hard,

but didn't place or show.

But just remember one thing, dear –

a fact so very true.

If I were a perfect human being,

would I have a need for you?

This poem was selected for publication in "Our Twentieth Century's Greatest Poems" in 1982 by World of Poetry Press.

THE WISH

Not long ago, as I went my way
   down a lonely path on a lonely day,
suddenly from behind a tree
   a little man jumped out at me.
He said, "I have a wish for you.
   I'll give ye one, can't give ye two.
This wish I give is strong as granite;
   'twill last forever, so carefully plan it.
I'll be here tomorrow day.
   Be here at three or I'll be gone away.
Not a minute before and not a minute past,
   if you want your wish to last and last.
And one thing more, you can tell no one
   or your business with me is over and done."

Then as quick he came he was quicker gone,
   and in disbelief I wandered on.
All that night and without a wink
   I sat by candlelight to think.
I pondered many a lavish thought
   while in fantasy my mind was caught.
Then just before the day anew
   it came to me what I would do.
All that day, clear up to two,
   the excitement within me grew and grew.
Then quickly I returned at three
   to the place where he'd be meetin' me.
And there in that lonely path he stood
   just as he promised me he would.

"So tell me, lad, your wish this day.
  I'll grant the thing and be on me way."
"Sir," said I, " I've thought this through,
  and what I want is to go with you.
To see the joy your wishes bring
  would cause my heart and soul to sing."
"So you want to go with me," he said.
  "Are you daft me boy? Has your brain gone dead?"
Then a serious expression crossed his face,
  and with hands behind him he began to pace…
back and forth, from tree to tree,
  occasionally stopping to look at me.
Suddenly he turned with a jerk
  and smiled at me; 'twas almost a smirk.
"All right then, lad. The thing is done.
  You and I will go as one.
But remember this, you can return here never;
  for this wish I grant 'twill last forever."

A hundred years have passed since then,
  and oh, the places I have been.
I travel with my dear friend, Shaun.
  Oh, by the way…he's a leprechaun.

THE QUIET WAY

We walked along the quiet way,
    just the five of us alone,
and experienced a warm togetherness
    that we have rarely known.
With ageless mountains above our heads
    and cool winds through autumn leaves,
we sensed a strange contentment there
    that put all our cares at ease.
We were Mother Nature's privileged guests
    on that crisp October day
with man's depressing asphalt world
    just a few short miles away.
While bending over crystal streams
    with abundant life endowed,
I felt a burning deep within
    and nearly cried aloud.
Oh, Lord, if only I could know
    this beauty every day,
all the worldly goods that I possess
    I would gladly give away…
just to walk this way, the five of us,
    knowing we could be
where the mountains tower overhead
    and the winds flow gently through the trees.

THEY DREAM

Yes, they dream...
those wonderful silver-haired warriors.
Warriors because they have fought the many battles of life
and reached their golden years.
They dream of times long ago.
They remember a less complicated world,
when a man was a man
and a woman was a lovely thing to be respected.
They dream of honor and a time when a handshake
was all the contract a man needed;
a time when a man's word was his most precious possession.
They dream of warm summer afternoons and ice cream socials,
of the county fair and the excitement of a circus coming to town.
They dream of mom and dad,
and a time when parents were in control.
They dream of a time when sneaking out behind the barn
to smoke corn silk was considered unacceptable behavior,
and a trip to the woodshed was the order of the day.
They dream of a time when hard drugs were unheard of,
and a woman's ankle was something to behold.
They remember dad's razor strap that hung on the back
of the bathroom door,
and every effort was made by all to see that it stayed there.
Yes, all of these things are dear to the hearts
of those wonderful silver-haired warriors.
These sweet people are lovely in my eyes.
I respect them
for the knowledge and experience they have passed on.
I pray we receive these gifts they so freely share,
and that we have the good sense to use them wisely.
Let us respect each other as in times gone by.
Let us long for a time when a couple's first kiss
could take place on a front porch swing,
and marriage is again held dear to our hearts.
Yes, take us back, my elderly friends,
and let us see how it once was...and oh, that it could be again.

HERITAGE

America the beautiful!
America the great!
What's happening to this land of ours?
Lord, what will be her fate?

So few salute the flag these days;
no hand upon the heart.
So many do not care, dear God,
and it's tearing her apart!

When was the last time that you saw
Old Glory wave on high?
Did your heart beat loudly within your chest?
Did teardrops fill your eyes?

Did you think of those who gave their lives?
So many died in pain.
Did you pray, "Dear Lord, don't let our men
have fought and died in vain."

We are the greatest country
this old world has ever known.
From Plymouth Rock's small colony
into a nation we have grown.

Do you think that such a heritage
should be allowed to wither and die…
or should "God Save America!"
become our battle cry!

STAND FAST, AMERICA!

Praise God for America – freedom for all!

She might stumble, but she won't fall.

Raise up Old Glory, our flag on display,

and back our great heritage every inch of the way!

Bring up the cannon; see the rockets' red glare.

Stand fast, America! There's victory in the air.

And bring forth her warriors. Leave her enemies in awe.

She might stumble, but she won't fall.

And here then her children – their future to see,

so steadfast Americans they'll want to be.

Let the word go forth across this great land

from Alaska's frozen shores to Hawaii's warm sands.

Let them know all Americans have answered the call.

She might have stumbled, but she'll never fall!

ODE TO ROBERT

Dear Robert, we know what you tried to do

as a precaution against the dreaded flu.

You thought that when you took that shot –

the germs, when they came, could enter not.

But look at you now, all piled up in bed

with fever in your body, and an ache in your head.

Bob, we know you're an employee so true.

But …we wouldn't pay a dollar for a case of the flu!

This poem was written in 1976 to a coworker who paid a dollar to take the flu shot at his place of employment, and he came down with the flu and missed a week of work.

FRUSTRATION

I've tried so hard

to write again,

but nothing seems to fit.

I think the best thing

for me now

is to break my pen and quit.

(I am so glad he did not give up.)

THE GRIEVING

I've been among the grieving mass.
  I've seen poor hearts that break like glass…
trembling hands and crystal tears,
  and minds so full of doubts and fears.

Time slowly passes, nearly standing still…
  like an evening shadow across a lonely hill.
Time can be cruel, taking a painful toll
  as it tears at the hearts of grieving souls.

I've often wished that I could say
  some tender words their pain to stave.
But words alone cannot relieve
  the pain inside of those who grieve.

So I wait and hope that in some way
  for them will come a better day.
Perhaps someone the grieved to tell:
  the worst is past and all is well.

"Dedicated to those who wait for word of a sick or injured loved one."

FAMILY AND FRIENDS

A FATHER'S DELIGHT

"It's a boy!" the nurse says.
All at once I'm a Dad –
the father of a son...
Oh, how it makes my heart glad!

He's entrusted to me now.
God sent him to me.
I must plan for the future
and what God would have him be.

There'll be times when he's good,
and times when he's bad.
But you see – that's the reason
God made me his Dad.

I must teach him what's right
and point out what's wrong,
and through the hardships of life
kind of guide him along.

Yes, coach your son, Dad,
and be his best friend.
And your reward, Pop?
He'll be a man in the end.

DID YOU EVER?

Did you ever look into a little girl's eyes
and know that your heart she had won,
or watch an elderly couple as they dance
at the wedding of their only grandson?

Did you ever stand in the warm summer rain
as the drops spatter soft on your face,
or escort your daughter to church Sunday morn
in her buttons and ribbons and lace?

Did you ever watch as a butterfly floats
on a wind that you cannot see,
or a spider as it spins its silken web
at the base of a giant oak tree?

Did you ever lie watching your Love as she sleeps
and feel the tears beginning to swell,
as you remember the day when she first came your way
and you fell under love's tender spell?

Did you ever stop to think of these things
that happen every day?
Or do you hurry yourself through a daily routine
and let Life slowly trickle away…?

MY LITTLE PRINCESS

There's a tear in my eye
as I lay her in bed
and touch the soft curls
on my little girl's head.

I look at her face…
Oh, God! I do love her so!
And I dread the day
when her own way she must go.

I touch her sweet hands
and her tiny little feet
and at that very moment
my heart skips a beat.

Yes, I will protect her
and guide her through life
'til on some distant day
she'll become some young man's wife.

As I leave her room,
my heart happy and free,
my little girl says:
"Daddy, will you cuddle me?"

SON

You know, I was there when you were born.
Many memories I recall…
A brand new life,
A little boy,
A babe so very small.

I remember plans that I had made,
and I thought of all that I'd do.
I would work very hard just to acquire
the things I would give to you.

I watched you grow as the years went by
with a father's love so deep.
And many nights I've thought of you, son,
as tears put me to sleep.

I've ached inside when you were ill,
and I'd be close by where you lay;
and I'd pray: "Dear Lord, give me his pain,
and let him go out and play."

Now, my son, the time has come.
So soon you'll be a man.
But nothing's changed…
I love you so,
and I'll do all for you I can.

HEAVEN SENT

I call him "Dude" but some call him "D,"
and no words can express what he means to me.

He came into my life about two years ago.
Dear God in heaven, I love this child so.

It makes my heart glad when he reaches for me,
and I'm the proudest grandfather you'll ever see.

Blue eyes and blonde hair, kind of short but not thin;
powerful legs and one foot that slightly turns in.

He loves to play ball, and I'm sure proud of that.
And he does very well if he has the right bat.

Sometimes he gets tired when the day is at end.
He'll say: "Rock me, Grandpa"… my little heaven-sent friend.

So he climbs on my lap and lays his head on my chest,
and we both settle down for a well-deserved rest.

We are so close. His heart beats with mine…
my "Dude," my "D," my daily sunshine.

SCOTTY

The first one to come – the first one to go;
not yet to heaven,
but to challenge the foe.

I'm so very frightened, yet I'm so very proud.
Though my lips may say nothing –
my heart cries it aloud.

Where are you going, beloved grandson?
How far will you travel
before you are done?

What things will you see as you travel the land?
Will you walk on green grasses,
or will you trod the hot sands?

Just always remember this old man loves you so,
and I'll be right there beside you
wherever you go.

So when you get home, we'll sit down one to one
and talk of your travels
until night hides the sun.

This poem was written to our oldest grandson just before his twenty-third birthday. Scotty had joined the United States Army in 2007 and was heading for boot camp at Ft. Leonard Wood, Missouri.

"PAPPY ROE"

Never before
      have I met a man
      quite like Pappy Roe.

If you walked into hell
      and needed him,
      he wouldn't hesitate to go.

If he calls you friend,
      he means just that;
      and he'll never let you down.

He'll be right there
      to lend a hand
      when others can't be found.

He'll tell the truth
      no matter what!
      his word is as good as gold.

But if you break a promise,
      or lie to him,
      it won't take him long to get you told.

I've seen him laugh,
      and I've seen him cry.
      I've seen him up and down.

But believe me, friend,
      there's not a better man
      on this earth that I have found.

"Pappy Roe" was about twenty years Gary's senior. They worked together for many years in a stressful environment and were best friends… like brothers. When Gary presented this poem to Pappy in 1991, he cried elephant-sized tears. Pappy was as tough as nails with the heart soft as a kitten. Gary preceded Pappy in death by fourteen months.

SACRED REFLECTIONS

IN THE BEGINNING

God made a man – made without sin.
God gave him paradise that he could live in.

God saw that man was all alone,
 so He made a woman; they would be as one.

The man was called Adam, the woman Eve.
The happiness they shared no one would believe.

But God had a rule that they must live by,
and if it was broken then they must both die.

There was a beautiful tree within paradise,
a tree we all know as the Tree of Life.

Now the fruit from this tree was an inviting treat.
But this was God's rule: "Thou shalt not eat."

Now the Devil moved in on this beautiful land.
He said to himself: "Think I'll take a hand."

So he tempted Eve until she gave in.
She ate of the fruit…and there began Sin.

She gave it to Adam; he ate of it too.
They had broken God's law – what were they to do?

Then God came down to talk with the pair,
but neither of them did he see anywhere.

God called out to Adam: "Why do you hide?
Is it because you've deceived me? You've disobeyed? You've lied?"

So God put Adam to work in the field
and Eve bearing children, in pain she would yield.

So now you can see how Sin got its start –
they put, for one moment, God out of their heart.

A NEED TO LOVE

Lord, I have known so many people in my life.

    Some I have wanted to hate,

        but could not.

    Some I have wanted to help,

        but they would not let me.

Lord, when I reach out in love,

    I pray I will grasp the hand

        of someone reaching back.

NOT VERY BIG AT ALL

Did you ever stop to think
how small you really are,
or how far it is from this Earth of ours
to the nearest shining star?

You know, you're just a tiny speck
on this globe called Mother Earth;
and I think sometimes we exaggerate
ourselves in terms of worth.

I have known so many people
who thought that they were great,
but when asked to help their fellow man
they seemed to hesitate.

They worship only one thing –
their god…the dollar bill.
They think that every need in life
their money will fulfill.

These people have my pity,
for they're missing all that's good;
and I would help them understand
if I thought they really would.

I have looked toward the heavens
on nights when the sky was clear.
My heart would race within my chest.
My mind would fill with fear.

I felt so very tiny,
so unimportant, so small.
For compared to God's great universe,
I'm not very big at all.

A MAN DIED

Lord, today a man died…suddenly.

He was my friend,

and I loved him.

My heart is saddened,

and I am burdened with guilt

for I did not tell him about You.

Lord, please help me

deal with the sadness and pain

that weighs so heavily

on my soul.

For I fear this shall haunt me

all the days of my life.

THE SOURCE

Dear Lord, I have a problem here.
Would You spend some time? Could You lend an ear?
I'm on my knees, my hands held high.
Please, dear Lord, don't pass me by.

I would talk with You. Oh, I need to so.
There's so many things I would have You know.
My aching heart cries from within
to be freed of this burden, misery and sin.

I've searched for the answer most of my years.
I've shed so many needless tears.
Countless hours depressed and low
with no place to turn. No place to go.

I thought perhaps with wealth untold
I could buy the world with silver and gold.
But I found that happiness cannot be bought.
No man can give it, nor can it be taught.
No wise man has it. It's in no book.
And you'll not find it here, though you may look.

I've found that happiness is being free
and knowing my God is leading me.
Just knowing that I'm in His tender care,
I will forever be contented there.

OVERFLOWING

Lord,

You have filled me

with limitless love.

My want and need to care

overflows.

I cannot think of one

with whom

I would not gladly

share Your love.

Lord…

I must

be about

Your business.

A DARK VALLEY…AND LIGHT

I felt so down, so lonely. I felt so very sad,
and I didn't realize the true Friend that I had.

I fell to my knees, with bitter tears flowing free,
and cried out: "Sweet Jesus! What's happening to me?
I have not the strength to carry on
for my desire to survive is now all but gone.
There's an ache in my heart; my soul longs to be free.
Please, my sweet Savior, send your angels for me.
Take me to that place where tears never fall,
and where bent, broken bodies stand straight and walk tall;
where deaf ears again hear, and sightless eyes again see,
and the sick, broken-hearted roam happy and free.
Yes, show me, my Master, that great city You've made
where my spirit will soar, and I shall not be afraid."

Then softly He said: "My son, it's not yet to be.
For you must linger a while and witness for Me."

Gary dealt with clinical depression over the years. Physicians and medications helped somewhat. The Apostle Paul suffered with his "thorn in the side" and God chose not to remove it. So it was with the depression.

HIS FACE

I have seen the dawning

        of a new day.

I have watched the sun

        disappear behind lofty mountain tops.

I have watched a fresh summer rain

        as it danced across golden fields.

I have looked into the eyes

        of my child.

And there, Lord,

        amidst all this beauty,

I have seen Your face.

UNTIL

As I have lived

then, too,

I must die

at a time

Thou has appointed for me.

But until my time comes

I will prepare

for the end

with songs of praise

to Thee.

....BUT LOST!

It's been a long time since last I was here.
How many months? Oh, I guess it's close to a year.
What brought me today…well, I really don't know
for there were so many places I wanted to go.
Oh well, since I'm here I guess I'll just stay,
 then go where I please with what's left of the day.

Well, the preacher has started, and I guess I'm stuck;
but perhaps he'll be brief if I have any luck.
As I look at the pulpit and the preacher I see,
it seems he is talking directly to me.
It makes me uneasy…I squirm in my seat.
I wonder, could I make a hasty retreat?

Now the message is over; the invitation I hear.
But why am I shaking? What is it I fear?
I can't go to the altar. All these people would see.
And the thought they'd be looking is embarrassing to me.
Oh, I know God is patient. He has waited this long
for me to repent and leave behind what is wrong.

I know deep inside I really must go,
yet another strong voice keeps whispering "no."
The choir is still singing. They're on the last verse.
Should I go or not go? Which one would be worse?
Well, I'll not give in. Not this time anyway.
There'll be another time…a more convenient day.

Gary had a coworker who was told if he didn't quit smoking and drinking then he would die from a heart condition. He stubbornly refused to change his lifestyle. He died in his 30s. Gary wrote this poem with his coworker in mind.

EERIE IMAGININGS

Gary was born in the month of October. Autumn was his favorite season. He enjoyed volunteering to work in the United Way fundraisers (as pictured above).

Kids of all ages still remember the excitement of coming to our house for trick or treat because Gary would have a "haunted house" to entertain the kids and hand out candy.

THE AWAKENING

I had a bad dream just the other night,
    a dream of horror and unbelievable fright!
In my dream I could clearly see
    the dreaded Grim Reaper coming for me.
I could hear his great sickle as it swished and swirled.
    I could see his black cape hanging down in long furls.
I could see his red eyes as they gazed into mine,
    and his outstretched bony finger as he beckoned me nigh.
I could feel my backbone slowly turning to clay,
    with icy hands on my shoulders as he dragged me away.
His power overwhelmed me! I could not break free!
    The mighty Grim Reaper was destroying me.
Then a miserable life flashed before my dim eyes;
    and my throat barely gave up its weak, feeble cries.
"Oh, Lord! Please grant me a few more short years,"
    I humbly begged Him through emotion and tears.

Then, suddenly, I awoke – the awesome Reaper was gone.
    Sun shone through the windows, and breakfast was on.

THE GRAVEYARD

I walked along the graveyard
        late one summer night.
The moon was bright…quite eerie,
         as it glistened full and bright.
All was very quiet.
        I heard not a single sound,
except the distant howling
        of a restless aging hound.
Oh, I have heard the stories
        of those who walk the night,
and the poor souls who've seen them,
        and literally died of fright.
Of how the prince of darkness
        would cast his evil spell
and bring the demons near to him
        from the very bowels of hell.
And how he walks from grave to grave
        and seeks the sleeping dead,
then by his touch these sleeping ones
        would raise their rotted heads.
But these are only stories
        told by campfire light
to scare the little children
        so they won't sleep at night.

But wait! There's something standing
        by that weeping willow tree.
And now it's moving closer.
        It's coming straight at me!
Oh, how I wish that I could run
        but just don't think I can,
for this thing has grasped me tightly
        with fleshless bony hands.

Well, it's been two hundred years now
    since I was scared to death,
and I remember my desperate struggle
    as I breathed my final breath.
So don't go near the graveyard
    when the moon is shining bright,
for you may join the others here
    who also died of fright.

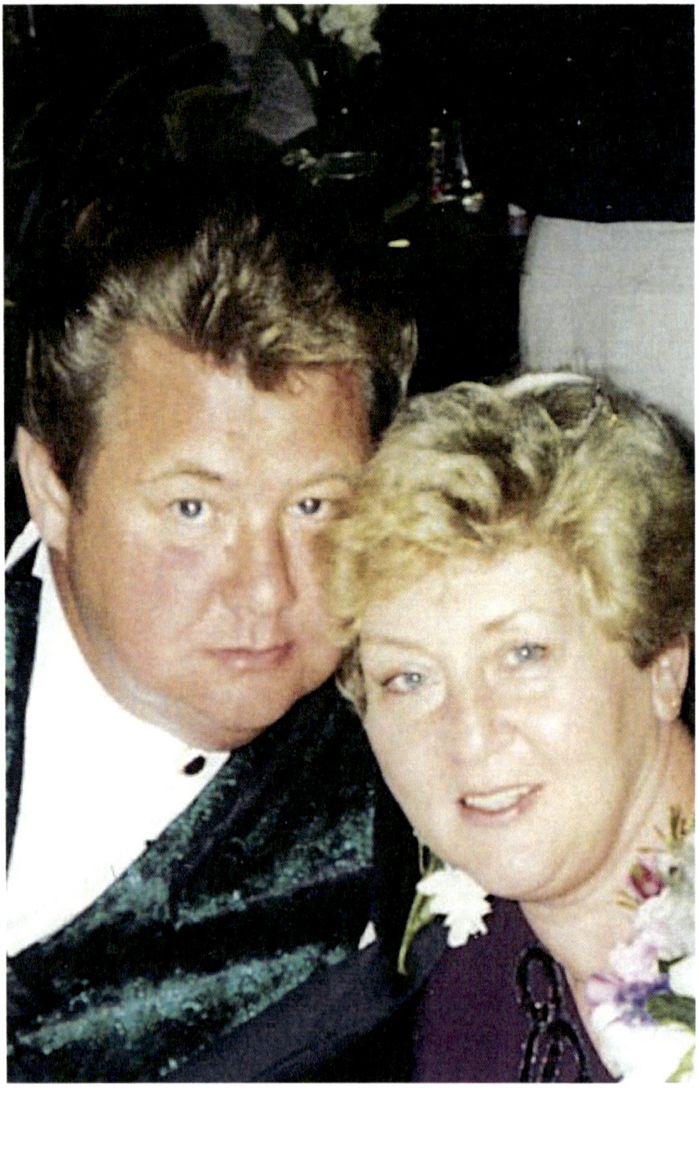

LOVE FOR A LIFETIME

MEANT TO BE

It was not as though we'd never met
for I'd known her quite a while;
and I saw beauty in her eyes
and a sweetness in her smile.

It was at a weekly high school dance
that this feeling came to me,
and I knew the first time that we danced
she was my bride to be.

I'd never felt this way before
and was not sure what to do.
I knew only that I loved this girl
with a love sincere and true.

We dated then for several months,
this sweet, shy girl and me...
this good ol' boy from Kentucky
and the young lady from Tennessee.

We married in the month of June...
the 29th as I recall.
We had little money, I had no job,
but still we had it all.

Now eighteen years have come and gone,
and we're still so much in love.
(That uniting of a man and woman
with God's guidance from above.)

He blessed us with three healthy children,
bright of mind and strong of limb;
and I feel our love is even stronger
just because of them.

Ya' know, I think we're happier now
than I thought we could ever be...
this good ol' boy from Kentucky
and the young lady from Tennessee.

MY LOVE

How do I love you?

I can't explain the way.

Nor can I explain the miracle

that night turns into day.

But I will say this to you, my love,

and mean it from deep within.

My love is as strong as any love

that there has ever been.

This poem was written for me on Mother's Day 1970.

THE CHAMBER

There is within my heart a chamber

that you, and you alone, occupy.

Inside, it is soft and warm.

The door is bolted tightly

so nothing may enter to harm you.

The chamber walls are made of pure love.

The bolted door is the tenderness I feel for you.

I could not remove you

for even I do not possess the key

that would loosen the bolt.

For you see, my love,

even though this chamber is mine…

I have no control over it.

And I am ever aware

of your sweet presence there.

HERE WITH YOU

If given a chance to return to Youth
        and live my life anew,
would I go back to such a time,
        or would I stay here with you?

This thought has played within my mind
        so many times before.
But I've always pushed it far outside
        and gently closed the door.

Old memories of times gone by
        and friends that time has lost
beckon me to return with them,
        no matter what the cost.

But although the Past is a beautiful time
        I would love to again pass through,
I think not, my love, but instead I'll remain
        right here - in this time - with You.

Gary wrote this poem for me in February, 1980. It was always my very favorite. I love the tenderness expressed in his choice of words. He was truly gifted.

Gary passed away suddenly on Friday, July 16, 2010. Early the following morning, unable to sleep, I was trying to organize my thoughts in preparation for the ten o'clock meeting with the funeral home director to make arrangements for the service. My son, Shawn, and granddaughter, Sarah, were with me. I told my son that I would like to have some of his dad's poems read during the memorial service. He thought that very appropriate as the poems reveal the heart of his beloved dad.

As I looked through some papers in the bookcase, I came upon two pages of notebook paper, folded, with familiar handwriting. The poem "Going Home" was written with a red marker (probably the only thing he could find to write with at the time he wrote it).

As Shawn and I read the words, we could hardly believe what our eyes were seeing. When had this poem been written? No one knows. There was no date. We had never seen this poem before. But the words were so prophetic. Did he know?! Did he "have a feeling"...a premonition...that he would be leaving soon? He had shared with a friend several weeks previously that he had an uneasiness about the surgery.

When Sarah awoke, I read the poem to her. She said, "Oh, Grandma! That makes me feel happy and not sad!"

The pain of not getting to say good-bye to the love of my life intensified the grief. But God in His tender mercy had allowed me to find "Going Home" at the moment of my greatest need; and it was as if He was allowing my husband to say "good-bye for now" to me. What a priceless treasure.

GOING HOME

I love you so very much, my dear, but I must say good-bye;

and it's so very hard to leave

with teardrops in your eyes.

But He is calling me away, and I know that I must leave;

and it breaks my heart to leave you,

knowing you will grieve.

But just remember this, my love. I'll have a mansion of my own,

and I will be much happier

than I have ever known.

There'll be no more pain to bear, and I shall not grow old;

and I shall watch God's children

as they play on streets of gold.

And when 10,000 years have gone, I'll have no less time to stay.

I shall never have to leave,

for it was planned that way.

Now I must board my chariot and fly toward the blue

where I shall wait and watch, my love,

until I can welcome you.